# Visions of Victory

# A Century of Sports Photography

Pindar Press, New York

Jane Livingston Associates, Washington, D.C.

The exhibition
*Visions of Victory:*
*A Century of Sports Photography*
at the Fernbank Museum
of Natural History, Atlanta, Georgia,
has been sponsored by
**Champion International Corporation,**
**The Paper Company,**
as part of its ongoing commitment to
supporting the arts in the United States.

Additional support has been received from
**MediaOne** and **Classic Sports Network.**

Edited by Dena Andre and Jane Livingston

Captions by Joe Guise

Jane Livingston, associate director and chief curator of the Corcoran Gallery of Art in Washington, D.C., from 1975 to 1989 and curator of modern art at the Los Angeles County Museum of Art from 1967 to 1975, is the author of numerous books, including *Black Folk Art in America; L'Amour Fou: Photography and Surrealism; The New York School: Photographs, 1936-1963; Richard Avedon, Evidence* and *Zelda, An Illustrated Life: The Private World of Zelda Fitzgerald*. She is currently preparing a major exhibition and book on the painter Richard Diebenkorn for the Whitney Museum of American Art and The Phillips Collection, Washington, D.C. She heads Jane Livingston Associates.

Dena Andre was co-owner of the Wolfe Street Gallery, Alexandria and Washington, D.C., from 1972-1979. As a member of the curatorial staff at the Corcoran Gallery of Art, Washington, D.C., from 1984 to 1991, she contributed to *The Indelible Image: Some War Photographs, 1847 to the Present; Odyssey: The Art of Photography at National Geographic; Changing Realities: Recent Soviet Photography* and *Songs of My People: African Americans, A Self Portrait*. Since joining Jane Livingston Associates in 1991, she co-organized the exhibition and book *Hospice: A Photographic Inquiry*, which is currently touring nationally.

Joe Guise joined Pindar Press in 1986 and currently is editor of the *Official Sports Guide of the Centennial Olympic Games* and the *Official NBC Viewer's Guide to the 1996 Olympic Games*. Pindar Press first published Viewer's Guides to the 1984 Olympic Games in Los Angeles and the Winter Games in Sarajevo (1984) and Calgary (1988) and was selected by NBC to publish the Official NBC Viewer's Guides for the Seoul (1988), Barcelona (1992) and Atlanta (1996) Games. Pindar Press also has produced the Official CBS Winter Olympic Guides for Albertville (1992) and Lillehammer (1994).

Cover photo: Rusty Kennedy,
*Jackie Joyner-Kersee, Barcelona, 1992*

Back cover photo: Jacques-Henri Lartigue,
*Rico, Gugy Kuhn, Lisbeth Thomas, Deauville,*
August 1917, © Association des Amis
de J.H. Lartigue, Paris

ISBN 0-918223-02-4
Library of Congress Catalogue Card Number 96-069502

©1996 Pindar Press, New York

A Pindar Press Book,
In association with Jane Livingston Associates

# Photographs by Sport
PAGE NUMBERS APPEAR IN BOLD

# Introduction

Photography and sports have evolved hand in hand for more than 100 years. The fascination of the idea of stopping time—glimpsing motion itself in its infinite forms—applies equally to viewing athletics and to creating photographic images. The two worlds, those of the athlete and the photographer, have evolved simultaneously in separate but overlapping universes, from a relatively primitive to an ever more sophisticated state.

One of the essential determinants of photography is *shutter speed*. A picture that required 30 seconds or more to be exposed looks quite different from one requiring only one-thousandth of a second. To understand this difference, one need only compare the racing crew image made in 1878 by William Notman (p. 6) to William Eppridge's 1986 *America's Cup* (p. 73). In the first, the boat's crewmen sit transfixed, waiting as quietly as possible for the camera to register their presence. The beauty of this photograph is in its details and in its stillness. In the second, the swiftly coursing yacht is caught gracefully in its trajectory; the boat and water together make a visual tracery that expresses gliding motion itself.

When we think of the increases achieved in sheer *speed* in such sports as sprinting, horse racing, skiing and auto racing, we are reminded that both human persistence and technology work to stretch the limits of athletic endeavor. Often the knowledge needed to improve sports performance is provided by the camera. Stopped-action images or continuous-action pictures, such as those pioneered by Eadweard Muybridge and Harold Edgerton, give us the scientific basis by which to advance the techniques of athletic performance.

In today's journalistic world, just as in art, photographers often embrace, rather than avoid, the blurred image which in the past was synonymous with photographic failure. We have learned that the "imperfect" photographic image can sometimes convey speed and the shapes movement takes more evocatively than the pristinely held split-second image. Technology and artfulness exist increasingly in synchrony; the same can be said of athletic endeavor. Photography is now accepted as an art form rivaling painting and sculpture. It is interesting to reflect on the recent ascendancy of ice skating as a competitive sport: Is it sport, or is it art?

The shift from large-format, glass-plate technology to the instantaneousness of 35mm film represents a journey spanning more than 70 years. In those same 70 years, virtually every sport we enjoy today—whether it's baseball, football, soccer, tennis, yacht racing, auto racing or gymnastics—has developed through advances in speed and technique into something that would have been unrecognizable (or non-existent) in the late 19th century. The significant breakthroughs in athletic achievement have paralleled breakthroughs in color photography. The four-minute mile was attained in 1954, at about the same moment that Ektachrome and Kodachrome color film were first beginning to be commercially viable color processes. From that point onward, revolutionary advances in athletics have kept pace neck and neck with the changing technologies of their documentation. Photojournalism throughout the last four decades has steadily increased its power to capture the aura of speed, finesse and audacity inherent in sporting adventure.

Now we are at a new and especially revolutionary threshold in the technology of photographic imaging. No longer does the printing, or even the capturing, of a picture-in-light rely on lenses and emulsions. We are entering the age of the computer-generated "photograph."

This exhibition and book represent the first time that the prints used are all made with digital images, generated from old-fashioned media (slides or prints) by scanning them with high-resolution equipment, and then altering, or "retouching" them, with computer technology using a special monitor. Once the images have been corrected to conform to their "original" states, they are finally printed out on the large, rotating drum of the Scitex printer. Each infinitesimal molecule of the ink's placement on the whirling paper is determined by a computer program taken from the original scan. The process, known as Iris printing, is capable of rendering subtle black and whites in literally millions of separate hues. All of the prints in this exhibition are printed with fine-art, archival inks that will last as long as, or longer than, even the most stable photographic prints.

*Visions of Victory: A Century of Sports Photography* has been organized for initial presentation at the 1996 Centennial Olympic Games in Atlanta. The coincidence of two 100-year celebrations—that of the modern Olympiad and that of the era of sports photography—seemed to call for a gesture of acknowledgment.

The project's conception was based on the simple conviction that the endeavor of photographing sports has been underappreciated in comparison to photography's other genres. We—the museum curators Dena Andre and I—combined forces with Harvey Rubin, Publisher of Pindar Press, to create a show that would rely equally on accepted art photography, anonymous images of sporting events and contemporary journalism. The exhibition was supported by Champion International Corporation, The Paper Company. We were assisted in the journalistic area by the photographer and photo-editor Rich Clarkson and in the artistic area by our museum colleague Frances Fralin. As the project developed, it seemed the perfect vehicle with which to join forces with David Adamson in pioneering the art of the Iris print exhibition.

The results are to be seen on the pages of this book.

Jane Livingston

*Boat's Crew, H.M.S. Pert, Naval Yard, Halifax, Nova Scotia. Commissioner's House. November 1878.*

**William Notman**
*Racing boat crew, HMS Pert, Halifax, Nova Scotia,* November 1878
Notman Photographic Archives, McCord Museum of Canadian History, Montreal

William Notman (1826-1891) was a Scotsman who emigrated to Montreal, Canada, and established one of the most prodigious photographic businesses in that country's history. Working in virtually every photographic medium of his day, including Daguerreotypy, collodion wet-plate and gelatin dry-plate techniques, and albumen and platinum printing. Notman travelled extensively in Canada, photographing people from all stations of life in diverse geographic settings. Besides working "on location," he created elaborate studio tableaux to simulate the outdoors. He claimed he could "build cottages, form sandy beaches with boats drawn up, erect tents, plant trees . . . form snow-wreathed plains or introduce a frozen lake or stream." He is one of the few photographers to have worked equally successfully in the studio and out of doors.

**Thomas Eakins**
*Double Jump,* 1885
The Franklin Institute

The Philadelphia artist Thomas Eakins (1844-1916) is best known as one of America's greatest painters. His meticulous and naturalistic approach to the human figure was assisted in great part by his photographic studies, both of single subjects, often nudes, and experiments in capturing human movement. It was Eakins who was instrumental in bringing the photographer Eadweard Muybridge to the University of Pennsylvania to pursue his motion studies; the two scientifically inclined artists influenced one another significantly. Long after Eakins was recognized as a master draughtsman, his photographs came to be valued in their own right as among the most artful of their era.

**Eadweard Muybridge**
*Boxers,* c. 1887
The Corcoran Gallery of Art, Washington, D.C.

Eadweard Muybridge (1830-1904) is equally known for his landscapes done in the western U.S. and his scientifically undertaken studies of people and animals in motion. Born in England, Muybridge came to America in 1852 and established a bookstore in San Francisco. In 1872, he was engaged by Leland Stanford to photograph his horse, Occident, at a gallop: Stanford had wagered that a horse moving at full speed would at some instants have all four feet off the ground. Muybridge's photographic efforts won Stanford's bet. Muybridge's so-called "animal locomotion studies," commissioned by the University of Pennsylvania, were begun in 1872. These hundreds of images were accomplished with up to 12 cameras, recording a variety of subjects ranging from pacing tigers to female dancers.

**Anonymous**
*Archer, Mongolia*, c. 1890s
Collection National Geographic Society

**Joseph Byron**
*Woman on Rings, Gymnasium,*
*Dr. Savage's School, New York*, 1899
Corbis-Bettmann

**Anonymous**
*Tennis Tournament, Smith College,* 1902
J. Paul Getty Museum

**William Henry Jackson**
*Golf in St. Augustine,* c. 1902
Library of Congress

William Henry Jackson (1843-1942), who began his career in the East as a photographic retoucher, became one of the leading American Western landscape photographers of the late 19th century. He was commissioned in 1870 to provide photographic documentation for the U.S. Geological Survey of the Territories, and proceeded, using mammoth-plate cameras, to develop a style at once descriptive and romantically sublime. In 1879, Jackson established his own studio in Denver and eventually published many of his own images with the Detroit Publishing Company, which he owned and which disseminated many of the important American photographs of the turn of the century.

**Baron Wilhelm von Gloeden**
*Wrestlers, Taormina, Sicily, Italy,*
c. 1903
Collection National Geographic Society

Baron Wilhelm von Gloeden (1856-1931) was born in Germany but settled in Taormina, Sicily, because of poor health. He learned photographic technique from a cousin in Naples and devoted much of his life to photographing the young men of Taormina. His openly homoerotic work was avidly collected by wealthy European and American esthetes. After von Gloeden's death, one of his main subjects, Pancrazio Bucini, became the trustee of some 3,000 glass-plate negatives. Because most of that trove was destroyed or damaged when they were impounded by a fascist raiding party in 1936 (the estate was subsequently acquitted of pornography charges), groups of prints have only emerged sporadically since then, including a number of works in the collection of the National Geographic Society.

**Anonymous**
*Fred Winters,* 1904
Missouri Historical Society
American Fred Winters finished second in the
all-around dumbbell contest at the 1904 Olympics
in St. Louis. The event, which had no weight
classes and is no longer a part of the Games,
required all competitors to try nine different
types of lifts, including the one-arm lift Winters
is attempting.

**Alfred Stieglitz**
*Going to the Post, Morris Park,* 1904
George Eastman House

Alfred Stieglitz (1864-1946) is perhaps the single most influential figure in
the history of American art photography. As the founder of a major New York
gallery called "291," he introduced a great deal of European Modernism to
the U.S. and encouraged young American painters and photographers to take
inspiration from them. His own photography evolved from a soft-focus
"pictorialist" style to a radically abstract body of work recording clouded
skies in moonlight that he called "Equivalents." Among his best known images
are the many portraits he made of his artistic protégée and lover, the young
Georgia O'Keeffe. Stieglitz's magazine, *Camera Work,* 1903-1917, remains a
monument in the history of photographic publishing.

**Anonymous**

*Dorando Pietri*, 1908

Hulton Deutsch Collection, London

The course for the Olympic Marathon was lengthened from 25 miles to its current peculiar distance of 26 miles, 385 yards at the 1908 London Games at the request of the British Royal Family, who wanted the race to start beneath Princess Mary's bedroom window at Windsor Castle and finish in front of Queen Alexandra's box at the stadium. Italy's Dorando Pietri was the first runner to enter the stadium, but he was disoriented. In fact, he started running around the track in the wrong direction until officials set him straight. Pietri collapsed on the track five times during that final lap, the fifth fall coming a few yards short of the finish. Jack Andrew, the organizer of the race, helped him across the line. As Pietri was carried away on a stretcher, the Americans lodged a successful protest to have him disqualified. John Hayes, a 22-year-old American who had finished second, was declared the winner.

13

**Charles Martin Conlon**
*Ty Cobb sliding into third base,* 1910
The Sporting News
Nicknamed "The Georgia Peach," Ty Cobb was born in Narrows, Ga., in 1886 and died in Atlanta in 1961. He still holds the record for highest lifetime batting average, hitting a remarkable .367 during his 24-year major league career (1905-1926 with the Detroit Tigers and 1927-28 with the Philadelphia Athletics). Cobb was one of the fiercest competitors in sports history. "I always went into the bag full speed, feet first," he once said. "I had sharp spikes on my shoes. If the baseman stood where he had no business to be and got hurt, that was his fault." In 1936, Cobb joined Babe Ruth, Walter Johnson, Christy Mathewson and Honus Wagner as the first players elected to Baseball's Hall of Fame.

**Lewis Hine**
*Playground in Tenement Alley, Boston*, 1909
George Eastman House

Lewis Hine (1874-1940) is perhaps best known for his tireless documentation of child laborers throughout the United States, which he commenced between 1908 and 1916 as photographer for the National Child Labor Committee. His interest in social reform combined with his prodigious photographic skills to create a great number of images that would become powerfully influential, but only after his death. Starting in 1905 with pictures of immigrants at Ellis Island and culminating in the *Men at Work* series made in New York in the early 1930s—including images of the Empire State Building under construction—Hine contributed a body of work that was first honored by members of New York's Photo League in the 1940s. Since then, his has become one of the most revered names in American photography.

**Jacques-Henri Lartigue**
*The Diving of Cousin Jean,* 1911
© Association des Amis de J.H. Lartigue

Like Wolfgang Amadeus Mozart in music, Jacques-Henri Lartigue (1894-1988) is known as the ultimate child prodigy of photography.
A member of a large, upper-class French family, Lartigue had already produced much of his best work by the age of 12. He was entranced
by the games and sporting activities of his family and friends and set out with his camera to capture frenetic or humorous movement,
especially people diving or falling, and airplanes, boats and racecars in motion. Although he continued to photograph in later life, he
devoted much of his mature energy to painting. Unlike Mozart, Lartigue is still most widely honored for his childhood achievements.

**James Van Der Zee**
*Basketball Team*, c. 1915
The Metropolitan Museum of Art

James Van Der Zee (1886-1983) is the most famous, and one of the most prodigious, of African-American photographers documenting their own environments in the early 20th century. Van Der Zee's childhood was relatively privileged; his parents—maid and butler to Ulysses S. Grant—made sure their son was educated in music and art. From 1916, when Van Der Zee moved to Harlem, until his death, he photographed African-American life in New York, covering ceremonial events such as parades, funerals, weddings and social gatherings. He also focused on local sports teams and street life and took many formal portraits. His style was highly artful and yet deeply vernacular, enabling a body of work that captures an entire era in American social history.

**Anonymous**
*Brighton Beach Automobile Races*, c. 1920
UPI/Corbis-Bettmann

**Anonymous**
*Jim Thorpe, Stockholm, 1912*
Allsport/Hulton Deutsch

Jim Thorpe, a Native American, won the decathlon and the pentathlon at the 1912 Olympics in Stockholm, setting records in both events. King Gustav of Sweden told Thorpe, "Sir, you are the greatest athlete in the world." Thorpe answered: "Thanks, King." Six months after his double triumph, it was revealed that Thorpe had been paid to play semipro baseball in North Carolina during the summers of 1909 and 1910. The International Olympic Committee stripped him of his medals for violating its amateur code. Thorpe went on to play pro baseball and also was one of pro football's pioneers (he was elected a charter member of Pro Football's Hall of Fame in 1963). In 1950, the Associated Press named him the greatest male athlete of the first half of the 20th century. He died in 1953, but, after much debate, his Olympic gold medals were returned posthumously to his children on Jan. 18, 1983.

**Jacques-Henri Lartigue**
*Grand Prix de l'ACF*, 1912
© Association des Amis de J.H. Lartigue

**Jacques-Henri Lartigue**
*Rico, Gugy Kuhn, Lisbeth Thomas,*
*Deauville,* August 1917
© Association des Amis
de J.H. Lartigue

**Anonymous**
*Red Grange,* 1925
UPI/Corbis-Bettmann
Harold "Red" Grange was the most famous football player of his
day. Known as the "Galloping Ghost," he averaged 182 yards
rushing per game during his three-year varsity career at the
University of Illinois (1923-25) and, during a memorable show-
down with rival Michigan in 1924, he scored four touchdowns in
the game's first 12 minutes on runs of 95, 67, 56 and 44 yards.
He went on to a successful pro football career with the Chicago
Bears and the New York Yankees and was elected a charter
member of Pro Football's Hall of Fame in 1963.

**Edward Steichen**

*Steeplechase Grandstand, Paris*, 1913
Reprinted with permission of
Joanna T. Steichen

Edward Steichen (1879-1973) had
as varied a career as any U.S.
photographer of his era. Born in
Luxembourg and established in
America in 1881, he began as a
"pictorialist" art photographer in the
New York circle of Alfred Stieglitz.
As a part of one of the greatest
movements in early photography—
the so-called Photo-Secession—he
came to know most of the
photographers and painters of the
American vanguard. After World
War I, Steichen continued to broaden
his photographic approach,
doing still lifes, portraits and
documentary style work, leading up
to his stint in World War II as com-
mander in charge of all Navy combat
photography. In 1947, Steichen
became head of the photographic
department at New York's Museum of
Modern Art; in that role, he organized
the watershed 1955 exhibition,
*The Family of Man*.

**Anonymous**
*Notre Dame's Four Horsemen*,
1924
UPI/Corbis-Bettmann
In the October 19, 1924 edition
of the *New York Herald Tribune*,
sportswriter Grantland Rice gave
the nickname "Four Horsemen"
to the Notre Dame backfield (left
to right): right halfback Don
Miller, fullback Elmer Layden,
left halfback Jim Crowley and
quarterback Harry Stuhldreher.
None of them stood taller than
six feet or weighed more than
162 pounds, but the quartet
helped Notre Dame compile a
28-2 record in the 30 games they
played for coach Knute Rockne
and led the Irish to the 1924
national championship.

**Anonymous**

*Suzanne Lenglen*, c. 1925
Corbis-Bettmann
French tennis player Suzanne Lenglen
was one of the world's most famous
athletes of the 1920s. She won five
straight Wimbledon singles titles
from 1919-1923 and added a sixth
championship in 1925. She also won
six singles titles at the French
Championships.

**Martin Munkacsi**
*Soccer Player, Budapest,* c. 1923
© Joan Munkacsi, Courtesy J. Paul
Getty Museum

By the time Martin Munkasci (1896-1963)
emigrated to the U.S. from Budapest,
Hungary, via Berlin in 1934, he already
was established as a successful sports
photographer and magazine and news-
paper editor. In New York, Munkacsi's
talent soon was recognized by the
influential editors of *Harper's Bazaar,*
Carmel Snow and Alexey Brodovitch,
who encouraged him to apply his
famously active, naturalistic approach
to outdoor photography to the disci-
pline of fashion photography. Munkasci
was almost single-handedly responsible
for bringing fashion work out of the
studio and into both daylight and
motion: his models ran and swam, and
sometimes seemed to fly. Today his
earlier sports photography and later
editorial work are equally valued for
their artistry and their innovation.

**Anonymous**
*Bobby Jones,* 1930
UPI/Corbis-Bettmann
Acclaimed as a conquering hero, American golfer Bobby Jones
rides down Broadway in New York City during a ticker-tape
parade honoring him for winning the 1930 British Open and
British Amateur titles. During his storied career, Jones won four
U.S. Open titles (1923, '26, '29 and '30) and three
British Open titles (1926, '27 and '30).

**Anonymous**
**Anonymous**
*Babe Ruth,* 1931
UPI/Corbis-Bettmann
George Herman "Babe" Ruth remains one of the
most recognized names in U.S. history. He was a
larger-than-life figure with the New York Yankees
from 1920-34 and was baseball's biggest box-office
attraction. "I won't be happy until we have every
boy in America between the ages of 6 and 16
wearing a glove and swinging a bat," Ruth once
said. Even though he was incredibly skilled at every
aspect of the game, Ruth's legend grew because of
his ability to hit mammoth home runs. He was
hitting 50-plus homers in a season during an era
when only a few players could manage 25. Ruth's
slugging average of .690, his ratio of one home
run for every 8.5 at bats and his total of 2,056
walks are all still records. And he is second in
career homers, career runs and career RBI.
"I coulda hit a .400 lifetime average easy," said
Ruth, whose career mark was .342. "But I woulda
had to hit them singles. The people were payin' to
see me hit them home runs."

**Anonymous**
*Gertrude Ederle,* August 6, 1926
UPI/Corbis-Bettmann
American swimmer Gertrude Ederle won a gold medal and two bronze
medals at the 1924 Olympics in Paris, but she gained worldwide fame
two years later by becoming the first woman to swim across the English
Channel. Here she stands covered with body-warming grease before
starting her historic swim, which took 14 hours and 31 minutes (almost
two hours faster than the men's record at the time).

**Underwood and Underwood**
*Preparing for the Games of the X Olympiad, Los Angeles, 1932*
Photography Collections/University of Maryland Baltimore County
The 1932 Olympics in Los Angeles were the second Summer Games on U.S. soil (St. Louis hosted the 1904 Games). Even the Great Depression couldn't prevent these Games from becoming the first to turn a profit. Approximately one million people attended the Olympics, and the stands were filled with Hollywood stars such as Will Rogers, Gary Cooper and Clark Gable.

**William Ritasse**
*Polo Players,* c. 1933
Courtesy Howard Greenberg Gallery

Though William Ritasse (1894-1968) spent most of his working life in Philadelphia, little is known about his early life or education. During the 1930s, he had refined his technique in industrial photography to the point that *Fortune* magazine regularly featured his images of subjects, ranging from Goodyear Tires to the construction of railroad cars. Ritasse, a prodigious technician and experimenter, combined a sophisticated command of the advanced forms of his day, including Cubism, Constructivism and Surrealism, with a command of "straight," or commercially descriptive, style. He was as capable of making highly imaginative combination prints—using darkroom techniques to juxtapose elements from more than one negative— as he was skilled in advertising and journalistic pictures, particularly in the area of sports. Ritasse is only recently beginning to receive wide recognition as a photographic master.

**Martin Munkacsi**
*Wrestling Match Between Szabo and Browning,
Harper's Bazaar,* 1935
© Joan Munkacsi, Courtesy Aperture, Inc.
and Howard Greenberg Gallery

**Alexander Rodchenko**
*Jockeys,* 1935
Courtesy Walker, Ursitti & McGinniss

Alexander Rodchenko (1891-1956) was
born in St. Petersburg, Russia, and by
1915 was a leading member of Moscow's
Cubo-Futurist artistic circle. Soon after,
Rodchenko turned his back on painting
and embraced photographic techniques.
Besides working in magazine journalism,
he allied himself with avant-garde
Russian filmmaking and cutting-edge
Constructivist imaging. Rodchenko
created a form of photographic montage
that combines reassembled elements of
both a *single,* and *several,* pictures,
resulting in images that at the same time
*depict* events, and *transform* them. This
approach has made him one of the most
imaginative photographers of athletic
endeavor who has ever worked.

**Anonymous**
*Jesse Owens Winning Olympic Gold Medal, Berlin,* 1936
AP/Wide World Photos
American Jesse Owens won four gold medals at the 1936 Olympics in
Berlin, a feat that was not equaled in track and field until American Carl
Lewis won four gold medals at the 1984 Games in Los Angeles. Owens won
the 100- and 200-meter sprints and the long jump in addition to running a
leg of the 4x100-meter relay. Nazi propaganda had taunted the U.S. for
having "black auxiliaries" on its team, and, of course, the German masses
were always being told by the Nazis that "all Negroes are inferior." Still,
the German people viewed Owens as the hero of the Games, and he was
repeatedly mobbed by fans seeking autographs.

**Anonymous**
*Sonja Henie, Garmisch-
Partenkirchen, Germany,* 1936
UPI/Corbis-Bettmann
Norway's Sonja Henie won 10
straight women's figure skating
world titles, starting at age 14 in
1927. She also is the only woman
to win three Olympic golds in
figure skating (1928-36). Henie
became a U.S. citizen in 1941
and took Hollywood by storm,
appearing in 10 movies. At one
time, she ranked third behind
Shirley Temple and Clark Gable
as a box-office attraction. Henie's
estate was worth more than $47
million when she died of leukemia
at the age of 57 in 1969.

**Alexander Rodchenko**
*Dangerous Jump,* 1936
Courtesy Walker, Ursitti & McGinniss

**Leni Riefenstahl**
*The Loges School Demonstrates
Skipping Exercises,
Berlin*, 1936
©Leni Riefenstahl Produktions

**Leni Riefenstahl**
*German Oarsmen,
Berlin*, 1936
©Leni Riefenstahl
Produktions

**Leni Riefenstahl**
*Art Diving, Berlin,* 1936
Library of Congress
American Albert Greene performs a dive off the three-meter springboard at the 1936 Olympics in Berlin. Greene won the bronze medal, while his teammates Richard Degener and Marshall Wayne finished first and second, respectively.

**Harold E. "Doc" Edgerton**
*Golf Drive by Densmore Shute,* 1938
© The Harold E. Edgerton 1992 Trust, Courtesy Palm Press, Inc.

Harold Edgerton (1903-1990) invented his stroboscopic light mechanism, with which he photographed events in split-second time, while a graduate student and assistant professor at the Massachusetts Institute of Technology in the late 1920s and early 30s. Objects such as a bullet hurtling through space were recorded in perfect focus with a flash of light as brief as one three-millionth of a second. In his hands, a drop of milk became a perfect tiara-shaped form, a cleated shoe denting a football was memorialized for all time and a golf swing was transformed into a sculpture in light. Edgerton, who taught at MIT until 1968, continued for decades to refine his high-speed experimentation with light and motion, combining a searching scientific curiosity with a remarkable artistic sensibility.

**Charles Martin Conlon**
*Ted Williams, Boston Red Sox,* 1939
The Sporting News
Ted Williams is the last player to hit .400 for a season, compiling a .406 mark in 1941. His career on-base percentage of .551 is still a record. Hitting a baseball, Williams often points out, is arguably the most difficult task in all of sports: "It's the only endeavor I know of where a man can succeed three times out of 10 and be considered a good performer." Williams did slightly better than that, averaging .344 during his career. "My primary goal as a player," Williams once said, "was to have people say, 'There goes Ted Williams, the greatest hitter who ever lived.'"

Charles M. Conlon (1868-1945) has been called the greatest baseball photographer who ever lived. Born in Albany, New York, he became a newspaperman early on, moving to New York City in 1900 to work at the *New York Evening Telegram*. Conlon became a lifelong baseball fan. In 1904, he started bringing his cumbersome glass-plate camera equipment to the Polo Grounds to photograph the New York Giants and never looked back. By 1920, Conlon was staff photographer for *Baseball Magazine*; throughout the 20s and 30s, he worked tirelessly in the baseball parks of New York. He is the photographer most consistently represented in the Baseball Hall of Fame. But he never achieved real fame; rarely in his lifetime did his name accompany his published works. It is a telling symptom of his times that, of the thousands of baseball photographs he produced, not one shows a black athlete.

**Anonymous**
*Lou Gehrig, Yankee Stadium,* July 4, 1939
UPI/Corbis-Bettmann
Before Cal Ripken, Jr. of the Baltimore Orioles broke his long-standing record in 1995, Lou Gehrig of the New York Yankees earned the nickname "Iron Horse" by playing in 2,130 consecutive games. The streak came to an end early in the 1939 season when it was discovered he had amyotrophic lateral sclerosis, a disease that now bears his name. On July 4, 1939, before 61,808 fans at Yankee Stadium, a tearful Gehrig, who knew he was dying, uttered the immortal phrase, "Today, I consider myself the luckiest man on the face of the Earth." Gehrig retired with a lifetime batting average of .340. He belted 493 homers (including a record 23 grand slams), and his slugging average of .632 is third on the all-time list behind Babe Ruth and Ted Williams. Gehrig helped the Yankees win six World Series titles during his 17-year career (1923-39). He was elected to Baseball's Hall of Fame in 1939 and died, at age 37, in 1941.

**Russell Lee**
*Contestant Mounting a Bucking Bronc at the Bean Day Rodeo,* 1939
Farm Security Administration Collection, Library of Congress

Russell Lee (1903-1985) began the work which made him famous by recording life in the streets of New York with a 35mm camera. By 1936, he was skilled enough to be brought into Roy Stryker's Depression-era photographic project, known as the Farm Security Administration. Lee's compassionate humanism continued to characterize his work in far-flung theaters of World War II, and in various segments of American society, from Japanese internment camps to coal miners and from tenant workers to minor league baseball players. Lee, who taught for many years at the University of Texas at Austin, worked in both color and black and white, achieving equal mastery in both media.

**Harold E. "Doc" Edgerton**
*Rodeo,* 1940
© The Harold E. Edgerton 1992 Trust,
Courtesy Palm Press, Inc.

**Harold E. "Doc" Edgerton**
*Swirls and Eddies of a Tennis Stroke*, 1939
© The Harold E. Edgerton 1992 Trust,
Courtesy Palm Press, Inc.

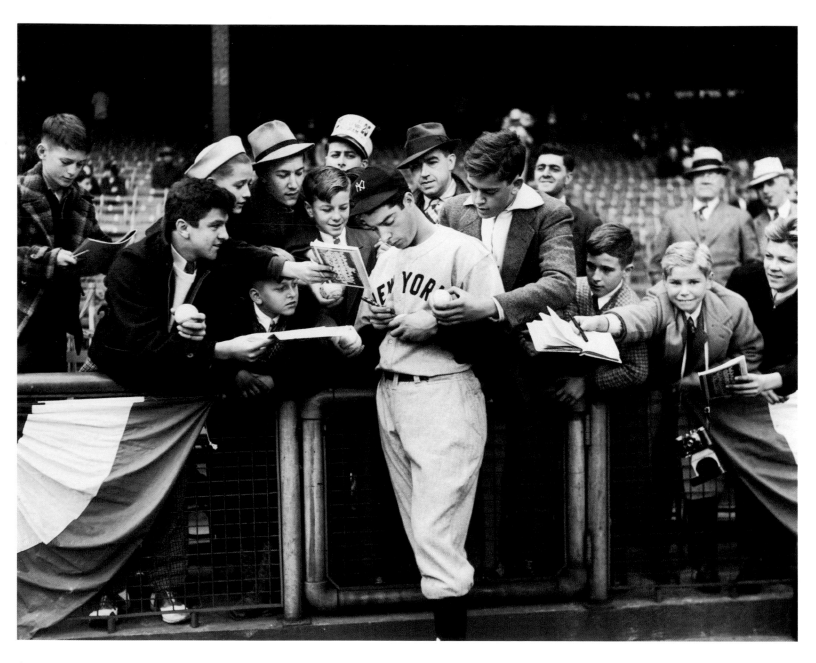

**Anonymous**
*Joe DiMaggio*, c. 1941
UPI/Corbis-Bettmann
Few played the game with more grace, fluidity and style than New York Yankees centerfielder Joe DiMaggio. His 56-game hitting streak during the 1941 season still stands as one of baseball's greatest achievements. Although he boasts many accomplishments—he played in 10 World Series during his 13-year career (1936-42 and 1946-51)—he was just as revered for the class and dignity he displayed while going about his job. "There is always some kid who may be seeing me for the first or last time," he once said. "I owe him my best."

**Arthur Rothstein**
*Baseball Game, Dailey, West Virginia,* 1941
Farm Security Administration Collection, Library of Congress

Arthur Rothstein (1915-1987) was a member of Roy Stryker's famous Farm Security Administration project. During the 1930s, Stryker engaged some of the finest journalistic photographers of the day to document Depression-era America; many of them, like Rothstein, were true artists and went on to forge major careers in photography. Rothstein photographed for the Office of War Information in World War II, and later became director of photography for *Look* magazine. He co-founded the American Society of Magazine Photographers and edited the seminal photographic journal, *Infinity.*

**Esther Bubley**
*Pin boy at a bowling alley, Washington, D.C.,* 1943
Farm Security Administration Collection, Library of Congress, Courtesy Kathleen Ewing Gallery

**Anonymous**

*Leroy "Satchel" Paige, Kansas City Monarchs,* 1942

National Baseball Library

Satchel Paige was one of the most dominant pitchers of his generation, but he performed in relative obscurity in the old Negro Leagues from 1927 to 1945. He stoically endured the disappointment of seeing his colleague Jackie Robinson precede him into the all-white major leagues. Paige finally got his shot with the Cleveland Indians at age 42 in 1948 and became the first African-American to pitch in the American League and the World Series. He played two seasons in Cleveland and three more in St. Louis before retiring. Then, at age 59, he made one last appearance in a major league uniform, hurling three innings of one-hit ball for Kansas City during the 1965 season. Paige, who was elected to Baseball's Hall of Fame in 1971, was fond of saying, "I ain't ever had a job. I just always played baseball."

**Anonymous**
*Althea Gibson, c.* 1945
International Tennis Hall of Fame,
Newport, Rhode Island
Althea Gibson made tennis history on August 28, 1950, when she became the first African-American to play in a major U.S. Lawn Tennis Association event by competing at a tournament in Forest Hills, New York. Until the 1950s, African-Americans were excluded from private tennis clubs as well as major tournaments. Gibson was finally invited to compete after becoming the top player of the all-black American Tennis Association. She broke the color barrier in tennis and cleared the way for other black athletes to compete in world-class events. In both 1957 and 1958, Gibson won Wimbledon and U.S. singles titles. She was elected to the International Tennis Hall of Fame in 1971.

**Gordon Parks**
*Spring football practice at Bethune-Cookman College in Daytona Beach, Florida,* 1943
Farm Security Administration Collection, Library of Congress

**Anonymous**
*Mildred "Babe" Didrikson Zaharias, c.* 1945
UPI/Corbis-Bettmann

Babe Didrikson qualified to compete in five track and field events for the 1932 Olympics in Los Angeles, but rules limited her to three. She chose the events in which she had set world records at the U.S. trials and won gold medals in the javelin and the 80-meter hurdles and a silver in the high jump (she tied the gold-medal winner, teammate Jean Shiley, but her technique was ruled illegal). Didrikson became a celebrity, not only for her talent but because she was such a colorful personality. Her comments during the Games were outrageous—she told athletes in other sports how she could easily beat them in their own event—but nobody doubted she could back them up. After the Games, Didrikson traveled the vaudeville circuit—she told jokes, sang, played the harmonica and performed a variety of athletic feats. She went on to become one of the best women's golfers in the world, winning 12 major tournaments, including three U.S. Opens (1948, '50 and '54). Didrikson died of cancer at age 42 in 1956, shortly after the Associated Press had voted her the greatest female athlete of the half-century.

**Gjon Mili**
*Louis-Walcott fight,*
1947
Life Magazine
Joe Louis and Jersey
Joe Walcott fought for
the world heavyweight
title in New York on
Dec. 5, 1947. Louis
won in a split deci-
sion. The two met
again the following
year, with Louis win-
ning by a knockout in
the 11th round.

Soon after arriving
in the U.S. from
Bucharest, the
Albanian-American
photographer Gjon
Mili (1904-1984) was
enrolled as a student
in electrical
engineering at the
Massachusetts
Institute of
Technology, where
he met and later
worked with Harold
Edgerton in perfecting
super high-speed
stroboscopic
photography. After
World War II, Mili
became a magazine
photographer, working
for *Life* and other
publications, and
created a kind of
hybrid of highly
technological strobe-
lighted motion
studies and a more
conventional,
naturalistic style
including portraiture.
He became especially
well known as a
photographer of
dance, theater and
sports.

**Anonymous**
*Bob Mathias Throwing Discus in Olympic Decathlon, London, 1948*
UPI/Corbis-Bettmann
At the 1948 Games, 17-year-old American Bob Mathias became the youngest Olympic decathlon champion in history. Four years later, at the 1952 Helsinki Games, he became the first to win consecutive gold medals in the event. He probably could have made it three straight in 1956—he was only 25 at the time—but the Amateur Athletic Union declared him a pro after he was paid to star in a movie, "The Bob Mathias Story." From 1967 to 1974, Mathias served as a Republican congressman from California's 18th District.

**Anonymous**
*Jesse Owens Racing a Horse at California's Bay Meadows Race Track, 1948*
AP/Wide World Photos
Even though he won four gold medals at the 1936 Olympics in Berlin and returned home to a ticker-tape parade down Broadway in New York City, American Jesse Owens never was able to capitalize on his fame. Unable to earn a substantial enough living competing or making related appearances, he was forced to perform in a series of unusual exhibitions, racing against horses, dogs and motor-cycles. Later in life, he became a hit on the lecture circuit by giving inspirational speeches.

**Anonymous**
*The Catch*, September 29, 1954
New York Daily News
With the New York Giants and Cleveland Indians deadlocked at 2-2 in the eighth inning of Game 1 of the 1954 World Series, the Indians mounted a rally. The American League champions, who had won a league-record 111 games that season, had two men on base when Vic Wertz stepped to the plate and launched a booming drive to deep centerfield. Willie Mays somehow tracked down the ball and made an incredible over-the-shoulder catch to preserve the tie. The Giants won the game in the 10th inning and went on to sweep the series.

**Anonymous**
*Jackie Robinson*, c. 1949
Cleveland Public Library
In 1947, Jackie Robinson broke baseball's color barrier by signing with the Brooklyn Dodgers. During spring training, several players signed a protest petition but were promptly told by general manager Branch Rickey and manager Leo Durocher that they gladly would trade any player who didn't want to be a part of the team. For weeks, Robinson's teammates would not sit near him in the dugout, and some even refused to speak to him. Robinson was quoted as saying, "I'm not concerned with your liking me. All I ask is that you respect me as a human being." Robinson hit .297 that first season, scored a team-high 125 runs and led the National League in stolen bases with 29. He was voted the NL Rookie of the Year and helped the Dodgers win the pennant, though they lost to the Yankees in the World Series. In 1962, Robinson became the first African-American elected to the Baseball Hall of Fame.

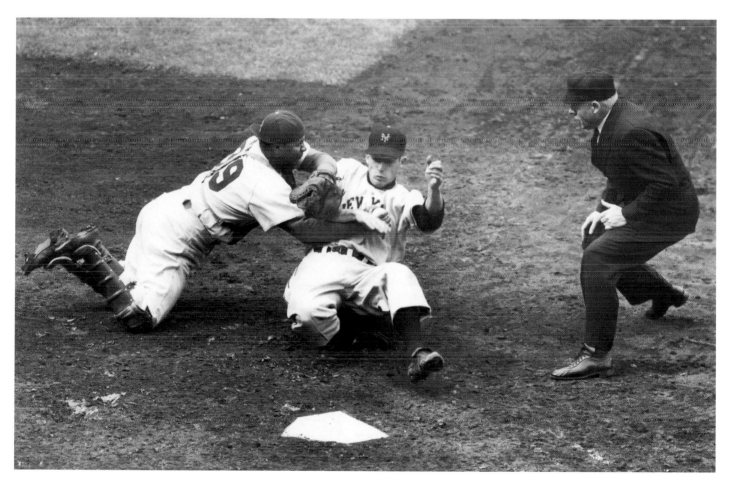

**Anonymous**
*Brooklyn Dodgers vs. New York Giants*, 1950
UPI/Corbis-Bettmann
Brooklyn Dodgers catcher Roy Campanella tags out New York Giant Jack Harshman at home plate. The Dodgers and Giants were arch rivals throughout much of the 1940s and 50s, a matchup made even more intense by the close proximity of the two teams.

**Anonymous**
*Joe Louis vs. Ezzard Charles,* 1950
AP/Wide World Photos
The fight took place on Sept. 27, 1950, in New York
and went 15 rounds, with Charles winning a unanimous
decision. Louis was trying to regain the title he had
held from 1937 to 1948. Charles was the heavyweight
champion from 1949 to 1951.

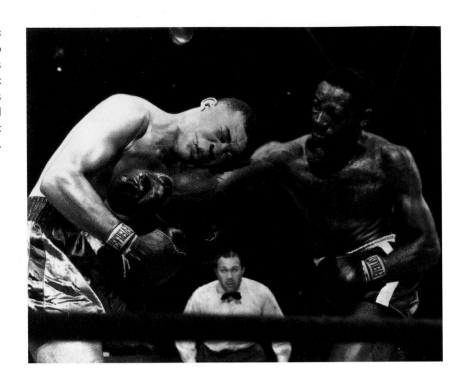

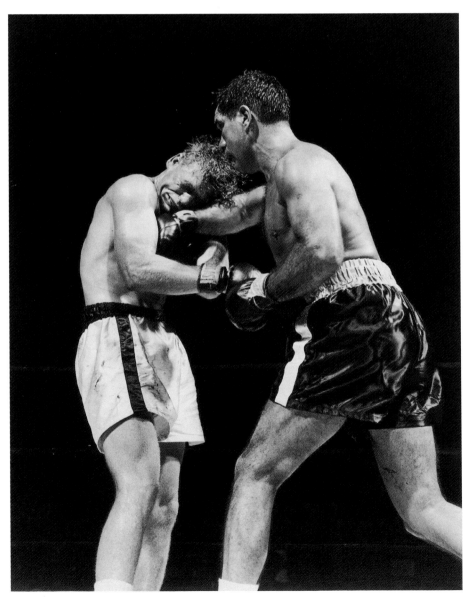

**Charles Hoff**
*Boxers,* 1950s
New York Daily News, Courtesy Howard
Greenberg Gallery

Charles Hoff (1905-1975) was a yeoman photo-
journalist who devoted virtually his entire career to
the *New York Daily News*. Trained in his youth as a
police and general assignment photographer, Hoff
stumbled into sudden eminence when his picture
of the *Hindenburg* going down in flames on May 6,
1937, instantly became one of the most famous and
widely reproduced photographs in history. In his
mature years, he gravitated increasingly to the
subject of sports, focusing especially on baseball
and boxing. Hoff is only now beginning to be
recognized as one of the most gifted of boxing
photographers.

**Anonymous**
*Roger Bannister*, May 6, 1954
UPI/Corbis-Bettmann
"When I went up to Oxford, I wanted to take part in sport," Great Britain's Roger Bannister once said. "I was too light for rowing, and I wasn't skilled enough for rugby. But I knew I could run." Bannister made history on this day by crossing the finish line in 3:59.4, thus becoming the first runner to break the four-minute barrier in the mile. "I suppose people will remember me for that," he said. "But my life has other strands." In 1973, as chairman of the British Sports Council, Bannister instituted track's first drug-testing program. He served eight years as Master of Oxford's Pembroke College (1986-94) and now, at 67, the neurologist edits medical journals.

**Anonymous**
*The Shot Heard 'Round the World,* 1951
National Baseball Library

That was the name given the home run hit by Bobby Thomson that clinched the 1951 National League pennant for the New York Giants. This view of the celebration at home plate is from behind the center-field wall. The Giants had won 39 of their last 47 games, including the final seven, to pull into a first-place tie with the Brooklyn Dodgers. The teams split the first two games of their playoff series, which set up the dramatic deciding game at the Polo Grounds on October 3. The Dodgers had a 4-1 lead going into the bottom of the ninth inning. The Giants closed the gap to 4-2 and had runners on second and third with one out when Thomson came to bat. Brooklyn manager Chuck Dressen replaced starter Don Newcombe with righthanded reliever Ralph Branca and chose to pitch to Thomson rather than walk him because Willie Mays was in the on-deck circle. Thomson lined a three-run homer over the leftfield wall to win the game. In the World Series, however, the Giants lost to the New York Yankees, four games to two.

**Anonymous**
*Jackie Robinson,* 1949
UPI/Corbis-Bettmann
Brooklyn Dodger Jackie Robinson was one of the best ever at stealing home (here he pulls it off against the Chicago Cubs in 1949, the year he won the National League Most Valuable Player award). Perhaps no athlete in history was scrutinized as much as Robinson. "He knew he had to do well. He knew that the future of blacks in baseball depended on it," Robinson's teammate Duke Snider once said. "The pressure was enormous, overwhelming, unbearable at times. I don't know how he held up. I know I never could have." And the legendary Willie Mays offered this simple tribute: "Everytime I look at my pocket book, I see Jackie Robinson."

**Robert Riger**
*Willie Mays stealing third base,* 1955
© The Robert Riger Living Trust, Courtesy James Danziger Gallery
"There have been only two geniuses in the world," the late actress Tallulah Bankhead once said, "Willie Mays and Willie Shakespeare." Dubbed the "Say Hey Kid," Mays was one of the most electrifying players of all time. Not only did he compile one of the game's most impressive stat lines during his 22-year career with the New York Giants (1951-57), the San Francisco Giants (1958-72) and the New York Mets (1972-73), numbers that earned him a spot in the Baseball Hall of Fame in 1979, but he did so with a flair virtually no other player could match. "Snider, Mantle, Mays—you could get a fat lip in any saloon by starting an argument as to which was best," legendary sportswriter Red Smith once said. "One point was beyond argument, though. Willie was, by all odds, the most exciting."

Robert Riger (1924-1995) grew up in Manhattan. After a stint in the Merchant Marine during World War II, he graduated from New York's Pratt Art Institute, and in 1950 began using photography as a tool for his drawings. For many years, Riger's distinctive sepia-toned sketches of sporting events were a standby in the pages of *Sports Illustrated*, appearing from its first issue in 1954. By 1960, when his first photography book, *The Pros*, was published, Riger was working as both an artist and a photographer. He soon added his writing skills to those talents and, at ABC's *Wide World of Sports*, became a producer/director of many award-winning television programs.

**Jesse Alexander**
*Peter Collins, Nürburgring, 1958*
© Jesse Alexander

**Justin Locke**
*Bull Fight, Mexico, 1953*
National Geographic Society

Justin Locke (1920-1979) was hired as a staff photographer by the National Geographic Society in 1947. During the short five years he worked with them, he travelled to and photographed in many parts of the U.S., Europe and Mexico, producing a body of work that is now regarded as among the finest sponsored by that institution. Though Locke never received wide recognition outside that context during his lifetime, much of which he spent living in New Mexico and Mexico and painting in watercolor, his photography is increasingly valued for its distinctively lyrical realism.

**Hy Peskin**
*Mickey Mantle,* 1956
Sports Illustrated
"Until I saw Mantle peel down for his shower in the clubhouse at Comiskey Park one afternoon, I never knew how he developed his brutal power, but his bare back looked like a barrel full of snakes." So wrote Dale Lancaster in the *Chicago Sun Times* in 1957. It was a blend of raw speed and awesome power that set Mantle apart from all other players. In 1956, the switch hitter won the elusive Triple Crown by leading the league in hitting (.353), home runs (52) and RBI (132). Mantle played in 12 World Series for the New York Yankees, leading them to seven titles, and still holds World Series records for most career homers (18), runs (42), RBI (40) and walks (43) and is second in hits with 59. He accomplished all this despite the fact his career was plagued by injuries. "On two legs," former Chicago White Sox second baseman Nellie Fox once said, "Mickey Mantle would have been the greatest ballplayer who ever lived." Although his life off the field was flawed, as he recounted in interviews before succumbing to cancer on August 13, 1995, Mantle represented the ultimate athlete to an entire generation.

**Anonymous**
*Gene Fullmer vs. Neal Rivers*, 1957
Corbis-Bettmann

**Robert Riger**
*Johnny Unitas, Yankee Stadium, New York,* 1958
© The Robert Riger Living Trust, Courtesy James Danziger Gallery
Universally recognized as one of the greatest quarterbacks in history, Johnny Unitas (19) led the Baltimore Colts to a 23-17 victory over the New York Giants in the 1958 NFL championship game, regarded by many as one of the greatest football games ever played. Unitas played for the Colts from 1956-72 and the San Diego Chargers in 1973. He was elected to the Pro Football Hall of Fame in 1979.

**George Silk,** *Hurdlers at the U.S. Olympic Trials in Palo Alto, California,* 1959, Life Magazine

**John Zimmerman**
*NHL Hockey*, 1962
Sports Illustrated
Toronto Maple Leafs goalie Johnny Bower
makes a save against the New York Rangers.

**Robert Riger**
*Wilt Chamberlain, Boston Garden*, 1959
© The Robert Riger Living Trust,
Courtesy James Danziger Gallery
All-time NBA great Wilt "the Stilt"
Chamberlain, then of the Philadelphia
Warriors, covers the ball on the famed
parquet floor of the Boston Garden in
a game against the rival Boston Celtics.
Chamberlain, who also played for the
Los Angeles Lakers during his 14-year
career, appears repeatedly in the NBA
record book, having led the league in
scoring seven times and rebounding
11 times. During the 1961-62 season,
he *averaged* an NBA-record 50.4 points
per game. That same season, on
March 2, 1962, he scored an NBA-record
100 points in a game against the New
York Knicks. Chamberlain even led the
NBA in assists in 1967-68, a rare feat
for a center. He was named MVP four
times and was elected to the Basketball
Hall of Fame in 1978.

**Walter Iooss, Jr.**
*Sandy Koufax, Connie Mack Stadium, Philadelphia, 1964*
Sports Illustrated

Sandy Koufax began his career as a Brooklyn Dodger in 1955 and moved with the team to Los Angeles in 1958. But it was the last six years of his 12-year career, 1961-66, during which he established himself as one of the most dominant pitchers of all time. During that span, Koufax led the majors in strike-outs four times, with a then-record 382 in 1965, and he won the ERA title every season except 1961. He won three straight Cy Young Awards (1963-66) and posted an incredible 129-47 record during those six seasons. "Trying to hit him then was like trying to drink coffee with a fork," former Pittsburgh Pirate Willie Stargell once said. And longtime manager Gene Mauch, who was with the Philadelphia Phillies back then, said, "[Koufax] throws a radio ball—a pitch you hear but don't see."

**Harold E. "Doc" Edgerton**
*Pole Vault,* 1965
© The Harold E. Edgerton 1992 Trust,
Courtesy Palm Press, Inc.

**Morris Berman**
*Y.A. Tittle*, September 20, 1964
Pittsburgh Post-Gazette
Hall of Fame quarterback Y.A. Tittle played for the Baltimore Colts (1948-50) and the San Francisco 49ers (1951-60) before finishing his career with the New York Giants (1961-64). Tittle retired just a few months after this game against the Pittsburgh Steelers.

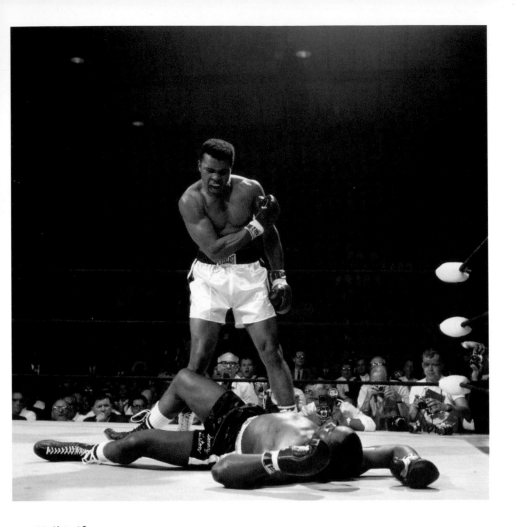

**Neil Leifer**
*Ali vs. Liston,* 1965
© Neil Leifer
In a rematch of a bout that had taken place just 15 months earlier, Muhammad Ali defeated Sonny Liston once again, this time by a knockout in the first round. "I call it the anchor punch," Ali said at the time. "People couldn't see it, it was so fast. If you watch the film, when I say, 'All right, I'm getting ready to hit him,' you gotta hold your eyes or you won't see it." Few athletes have ever matched Ali's worldwide popularity, and, in virtually every poll taken during the last 30 years, Ali is always listed as one of the most significant figures in sports history.

**Robert Riger**
*Muhammad Ali, Lewiston, Maine,* 1965
© The Robert Riger Living Trust, Courtesy James Danziger Gallery
On Feb. 25, 1964, Cassius Clay surprised the boxing world by taking the heavyweight title from Sonny Liston with a TKO in the seventh round. Shortly thereafter, Clay adopted the Muslim faith and changed his name to Muhammad Ali. Here Ali takes a 6:00 a.m. training run in preparation for the rematch, which took place on May 25, 1965.

**Rich Clarkson**
*Kareem Abdul-Jabbar (then Lew Alcindor), 1967*
© Rich Clarkson

In the first of three straight appearances in the NCAA Final Four, UCLA's Lew Alcindor, who would later change his name to Kareem Abdul-Jabbar, scored 19 points and grabbed 20 rebounds in a 73-58 semifinal victory over Houston. The Bruins then defeated Dayton, 79-64, to win the title, as Alcindor scored 20 and hauled down 18 rebounds. He was named Final Four MVP, an award he also won in 1968 (34 points, 16 rebounds against North Carolina in the final) and 1969 (37 points and 20 rebounds against Purdue in the final). Three days after UCLA's 1967 victory, the NCAA rules committee outlawed the dunk in an effort to offset the center's dominance. Still, he led the Bruins to an 88-2 record and three straight NCAA titles during his three-year career. Abdul-Jabbar then went on to play a record 20 seasons (1969-89) in the NBA and still holds records for most games (1,560), most minutes (57,446), most field goals (15,837), most blocked shots (3,189) and most points (38,387), among many others. He developed the most potent offensive weapon in the history of the game, the sky hook, which was virtually impossible to block.

**Rich Clarkson**
*Kareem Abdul-Jabbar*
*(then Lew Alcindor), 1967*
© Rich Clarkson

**John Dominis**
*Black Power, Mexico City,* 1968
Life Magazine
American Tommie Smith won the 200-meter sprint in world-record time at the 1968 Olympics in Mexico City, while his teammate, John Carlos, finished third. Later, at the medal ceremony, they stepped up on the podium shoeless, wore civil rights buttons and, as the national anthem was played, bowed their heads and raised one black-gloved hand in the black-power salute. They said their clenched fists symbolized black strength and unity, while removing their shoes was a reminder of black poverty in the U.S. It remains one of the most controversial moments in Olympic history. After the ceremony was over, both were ordered to leave the Olympic Village. Their visas were cancelled, and they were expelled from Mexico. Upon their return to the U.S., both had a difficult time earning a living, and neither was able to keep his marriage together. "Ours was not a political act, it was a moral act, and that is all right," Carlos once said. "When else can you do something like that? Only at the Olympics or when you land on the moon. Then everyone is looking at you."

**Tony Duffy**
*Bob Beamon, Mexico City Olympics,* 1968
Allsport/Tony Duffy
Some have called it the greatest single athletic achievement in history. That probably will be debated for quite some time, but American Bob Beamon's world-record long jump of 29'2½" certainly is a contender. Beamon surpassed the existing record by 21¾". Immediately after the jump, one of Beamon's opponents, 1964 gold medalist Lynn Davies of Great Britain, said, "I can't go on. What is the point? We'll all look silly." Then, he turned to Beamon and said, "You have destroyed this event." It wasn't until 1980 that anyone broke the 28-foot barrier, let alone the 29-foot mark. Beamon's record stood for 23 years until American Mike Powell jumped 29'4½" at the 1991 World Championships. "Mine was a jump way before its time," Beamon once said. "It almost made it into the 21st century."

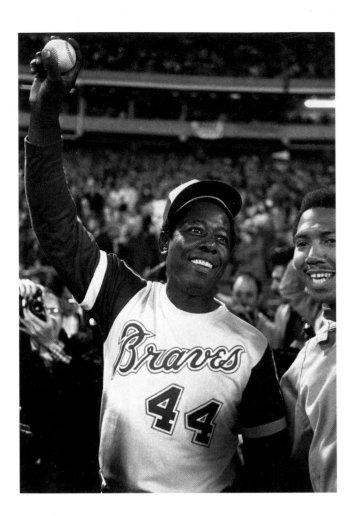

**Anonymous**
*Hank Aaron, Atlanta*, April 8, 1974
UPI/Corbis-Bettmann
Hank Aaron celebrates his record-breaking 715th career home run at Atlanta-Fulton County Stadium on April 8, 1974. Aaron surpassed the legendary Babe Ruth by blasting Los Angeles Dodger Al Downing's pitch over the leftfield wall. Although, amazingly enough, he never had more than 47 homers in a single season, Aaron hit a major-league record 755 during his 23-year career. He also is first in career RBI with 2,297. "Aaron's excellence," wrote Lonnie Wheeler in 1991's *I Had a Hammer*, "was not expelled in blinding bursts of energy but rather played out, patiently and inexorably, over a whole generation."

**Neil Leifer**
*Ali vs. Williams*, 1966
© Neil Leifer
Cleveland Williams was one of the hardest punchers Muhammad Ali faced during his fabled career. During their Nov. 14, 1966 bout at the Houston Astrodome, Ali was moving about the ring so quickly that some experts insist Williams landed just three punches during the entire fight. Ali knocked Williams out in the third round and would fight just two more times before serving a three-and-a-half-year suspension for refusing induction into the U.S. Army. "[The suspension] was very sad," said Ferdie Pacheco, Ali's longtime ring doctor. "It was like knowing a Mozart symphony or a play by William Shakespeare was somehow censored out of existence."

**Bob Coglianese**
*Secretariat winning the Belmont Stakes*, 1973
© Bob Coglianese
After winning both the Kentucky Derby and the Preakness, Secretariat captured the coveted Triple Crown, winning the Belmont Stakes by an incredible 31 lengths. The jockey in all three races was Ron Turcotte.

**Tony Duffy**
*Arthur Ashe, Wimbledon,* 1975
Allsport/Hulton Deutsch
Arthur Ashe defeated Jimmy Connors, 6-1, 6-1, 5-7, 6-4, to win the 1975 men's singles title at Wimbledon. Ashe was the first African-American male to win singles titles at the U.S. Open (1968), the Australian Open (1970) and Wimbledon. However, the most emotional moment of his public life came on April 8, 1992, when he reluctantly held a press conference to reveal he had tested positive for the HIV virus four years earlier. Ashe had contracted the virus from a blood transfusion during his 1983 open-heart surgery. Still, he remained an eloquent spokesperson for several causes, from fighting against apartheid in South Africa to serving as national campaign chairman for the American Heart Association. He died of AIDS-related pneumonia on Feb. 6, 1993.

**Neil Leifer**
*Joe Namath, Shea Stadium,* 1974
© Neil Leifer
Some say quarterback Joe Namath put the Super Bowl on the map by making good on his brash prediction that his AFL Champion New York Jets would upset the Baltimore Colts, champions of the more powerful and established NFL, in Super Bowl III (Jan. 12, 1969). The Jets came out on top by a 16-7 margin, and Broadway Joe, who played for the Jets (1965-76) and the Los Angeles Rams (1977), continued on a path to the Pro Football Hall of Fame (he was inducted in 1985).

**Anonymous,** *Nadia Comaneci, Montreal,* 1976, UPI/Corbis Bettmann
Nadia Comaneci forever will be linked with the number 10. The Romanian gymnast was just 14 at the 1976 Games in Montreal, where she earned seven 10s, the first perfect scores ever recorded at the Olympics. Even the scoreboard was not prepared for her success—it was designed to show 9.99 as the top score and only could list her mark as 1.00. Comaneci won gold medals in the individual all-around, the uneven bars and the balance beam. In 1989, she defected to the U.S., and, on April 27, 1996, she married former U.S. gymnast Bart Connor.

**Tony Duffy**
*Bruce Jenner,* 1976
Allsport/Tony Duffy
The 1976 Olympic decathlon was billed as a showdown between Soviet Nikolai Avilov, the 1972 gold medalist, and American Bruce Jenner, who was 10th at the 1972 Games. There was no bombardment of "Nikolai or Bruce?" ads prior to the Games, but it certainly was one of the more intriguing matchups. As it turned out, Jenner all but locked up the gold after eight events. Still, he pressed himself, even in the decathlon's grueling finale, the 1,500 meters, and set a world record with an overall total of 8,634 points.

**Heinz Kluetmeier**
*The Miracle on Ice, Lake Placid, New York,* 1980
Sports Illustrated
It remains one of the greatest upsets in sports history. The U.S. hockey team registered a 4-3 victory over the mighty Soviets at the 1980 Olympics in Lake Placid. Who can ever forget ABC's Al Michaels shouting, "Do you believe in miracles? Yes!" as the final seconds ticked away? The Soviets had won four straight Olympic golds prior to that contest and lost just one game in the process. But the Americans were not intimidated, even though they fell behind three times during the game. Team captain Mike Eruzione broke a 3-3 tie with 10 minutes to go, and the U.S. held on for the victory. Many who remember the wild celebration after that victory forget that the U.S. had to win one more game to capture the gold medal. Two days after the most memorable day of their lives, the Americans defeated Finland, 4-2. If they had lost that game, they would have ended up in fourth place.

**Chris Smith,** *Steeplechase, Newbury, England,* 1976, © Chris Smith

**Arthur Tress**
*Hockey Player, New York City,* 1976
Courtesy Houk Friedman, New York

**Jeffrey E. Blackman**
*Jimmy Connors*, 1982
© Jeffrey E. Blackman
Jimmy Connors has won more men's singles titles (109) than any other tennis player in history, a list that includes five U.S. Open championships (1974, '76, '78, '82 and '83), two Wimbledon titles (1974 and '82) and one Australian Open (1974). He also held the No. 1 world ranking for a record 159 consecutive weeks (July 29, 1974, through August 16, 1977) and was ranked among the world's top 10 for 16 years.

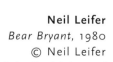

**Neil Leifer**
*Bear Bryant*, 1980
© Neil Leifer
Paul "Bear" Bryant is the winningest coach in the history of Division I-A college football, amassing 323 victories at four different schools from 1945 to 1982. He won six national titles, all at Alabama (1961, '64, '65, '73, '78 and '79). Bryant always said that when he stopped coaching football, he probably would die. The statement was sadly prophetic. He passed away on Jan. 26, 1983, just a month after coaching his final game.

**Chris Smith**
*Moscow Olympics,* 1980
© Chris Smith

**Dave Dieter**
*Sulky,* 1983
© Dave Dieter/The Huntsville Times

**David Burnett**

*Mary Decker, Los Angeles,* 1984
© 1996 David Burnett/Contact
Press Images

American Mary Decker looks on in
anguish as her chance at Olympic
gold in the 1984 women's 3,000
meters slips away. Just moments
before, she and Zola Budd, a
South African competing for Great
Britain, had collided, causing
Decker to lose her balance and
fall. With a pulled left hip stabilizer
muscle, Decker was unable to
continue—she was left on the
track, weeping from pain and
frustration, as the pack pulled
away. Budd finished seventh and
was disqualified, though she was
immediately reinstated when a jury
of appeal reviewed videotapes of
the race.

**Walter Iooss, Jr.**
*The Start, Los Angeles Olympics,* 1984, © Walter Iooss, Jr.

**Jose Azel**
*Los Angeles Olympics*, 1984
Aurora
An American runner named Thomas Jefferson drapes himself in the American flag after winning the bronze medal in the 200-meter sprint. Jefferson's teammates Carl Lewis and Kirk Baptiste finished first and second, respectively.

**Jeffrey E. Blackman**
*New York Jets vs. Buffalo Bills, Giants Stadium*, 1985
© Jeffrey E. Blackman

**Brian Lanker**
*Rhythmic Gymnast*, 1984
© Brian Lanker 1984
Rhythmic gymnastics made its Olympic debut at the 1984 Games in Los Angeles and remains one of the world's most misunderstood sports. These gymnasts perform *with* rather than *on* an apparatus, devising elaborate routines with balls, hoops, clubs, ribbons and ropes. The sport, which actually combines aspects of ballet and the more traditional artistic gymnastics, requires a tremendous amount of grace and agility.

## Herb Ritts

*Jackie Joyner-Kersee, Point Dume,* 1987
© Herb Ritts, Courtesy Fahey/Klein Gallery,
Los Angeles

Jackie Joyner-Kersee was born and raised in
the poverty-stricken town of East St. Louis,
Ill., in 1962. She and her brother Al, who
later would marry U.S. sprinter Florence
Griffith, lived with their family on a seedy
block with a pool hall and a liquor store, and
they once saw a man shot to death in front
of their house. "I remember Jackie and me
crying together in a back room in that
house," Al said, "swearing that someday we
were going to make it—make it out." Jackie
played volleyball and basketball at Lincoln
High, and she also ran track. She got out by
earning a basketball scholarship to UCLA,
but she also competed in track, specializing
in the long jump until her coach and
eventual husband Bob Kersee introduced
her to the heptathlon. Jackie took to it
quickly—she won the silver medal at the
1984 Olympics, missing the gold by just five
points, and then won the gold at the 1988
and 1992 Games. She also won the 1988 long
jump gold to become the first track and field
athlete in 64 years to win a multi-event and a
single event at the same Olympics. Pointing
out that her granddaughter was named after
President John F. Kennedy's wife, Jackie's
grandmother announced at her birth,
"Someday this girl will be the first lady of
something."

### Yann Guichaoua

*Bonnie Blair, Calgary Olympics,* 1988
Allsport/Yann Guichaoua

Speed skater Bonnie Blair has won more Olympic gold medals
(five) than any other female athlete in U.S. history. She started her
collection at the 1988 Games in Calgary by setting a world record
in the 500 meters and then followed that performance with
doubles (500 meters and 1,000 meters) at the 1992 and 1994
Games in Albertville, France, and Lillehammer, Norway, respectively.
Blair's victory in the 1994 500 meters also made her the first U.S.
athlete to win the same event at three consecutive Winter Games.
"I think every speed skater is nervous when they first step up to
that line," Blair's coach, Nick Thometz, said after the 1994
Games. "You don't go in with thoughts of falling, but they're there
lurking in the back of your mind. Bonnie is just the best at
channeling that nervousness."

**Gerard Vandystadt**
*Katarina Witt,* 1986
Allsport/Gerard Vandystadt
Competing for East Germany, Katarina Witt won Olympic gold in 1984 and 1988 and became the first woman since Sonja Henie in 1932 to win two straight figure skating titles. She caused a bit of a stir at the 1988 Games in Calgary by wearing costumes that some felt were too revealing. Witt has continued to perform skating exhibitions around the world and has served as a commentator on figure skating broadcasts. "It doesn't matter where I am," she said. "If I feel eyes on me, I'm better."

**Bill Eppridge**
*America's Cup, Australia,* 1987
Sports Illustrated
After losing the America's Cup to Australia in 1983, Dennis Conner skippered Stars & Stripes to a 4-0 victory over Australia's Kookaburra III and reclaimed the Cup.

**Walter Iooss, Jr.**
*Michael Jordan in the NBA Slam-Dunk Contest,* Feb. 6, 1988
Sports Illustrated
In 1996, Michael Jordan led the Chicago Bulls to their fourth NBA title in six years after a record-breaking 72-10 regular season (not bad for a former outfielder). Jordan continues to rewrite the NBA record books. He is widely considered the greatest basketball player of all time and is among a select group of players who have won an NCAA title, an Olympic gold medal and an NBA championship during their career. Despite all of his accomplishments, one of the signature moments of his career did not come during a game but rather during the 1988 NBA All-Star Weekend as Jordan captured his second consecutive slam-dunk title with a soaring, takeoff-from-the-foul-line jam.

**Kenneth Jarecki**
*Bobsled, Albertville Olympics,* 1992
© Kenneth Jarecki/Contact Press Images

**Heinz Kluetmeier**
*Chicago Bears vs. Philadelphia Eagles at Chicago's Soldier Field,* December 31, 1988
Sports Illustrated
It became known as the "Fog Bowl," with the Chicago Bears defeating the Philadelphia Eagles, 20-12, in the 1988 NFC Divisional Playoffs.

**Annie Leibovitz**
*Greg Louganis*, 1988
© Annie Leibovitz, Courtesy James Danziger Gallery
There is little debate that American Greg Louganis was the greatest diver in history. By winning the three-meter springboard and the 10-meter platform titles at the 1984 and 1988 Olympics, he became the only man to sweep both diving events at two different Olympics.

**Bob Long**

*Volleyball, US vs. USSR, Seoul Olympics,* 1988

Long Photography, Inc.

The U.S. won a thrilling four-set match over the Soviets, 13-15, 15-10, 15-4, 15-8, and won its second consecutive gold medal in men's indoor volleyball. Karch Kiraly, now the world's premier beach volleyball player, was captain and star of that U.S. team.

**Mike Powell**

*Florence Griffith Joyner,* 1988

Allsport/Mike Powell

American Florence Griffith Joyner emerged as one of the biggest stars of the 1988 Olympics in Seoul by winning gold in the 100 meters, the 200 meters and the 4x100-meter relay and a silver in the 4x400-meter relay. At the time, Flo-Jo's world-record mark of 21.54 seconds in the 200 meters would have been the national record for *men* in 69 countries. Even most NFL players could not run as fast as she did at the 1988 Games. Flo-Jo's physique was more well-defined and muscular than any other female athlete—her fanatical workout regimen included 1,000 sit-ups per day and four visits per week to the weight room, where she could squat 320 pounds. "If you want to run like a man," she once said, "you have to train like a man."

**Gregory Heisler**
*Carl Lewis*, 1988
© Gregory Heisler
Many have tried to write Carl Lewis' athletic obituary. Since he won four track and field gold medals at the 1984 Games, thus equaling the 1936 feat of the legendary Jesse Owens, countless runners around the world have been dubbed the next Carl Lewis. The trouble is, Lewis has refused to slow down. The American sprinter/long jumper won eight Olympic golds at three different Games—100m, 200m, 4x100m relay and long jump at the 1984 Games, 100m and long jump in 1988 and 4x100m relay and long jump in 1992—leaving him just one short of the all-time career record held by American swimmer Mark Spitz (1968-72), Soviet gymnast Larisa Latynina (1956-64) and Finnish distance runner Paavo Nurmi (1920-28).

**Michael Yada,** *Rhythmic Gymnasts, Seoul Olympics,* 1988, Long Photography, Inc.
Marina Lobatch (right) and Alexandra Timochenko (left) of the Soviet Union won the gold and bronze, respectively, at the 1988 Olympics
in Seoul.

**Annie Leibovitz**
*Magic Johnson,* 1989
© Annie Leibovitz, Courtesy James Danziger Gallery

As a sophomore at Michigan State University, Earvin "Magic" Johnson led the Spartans to the 1979 NCAA title by defeating Larry Bird's Indiana State squad, 75-64. The first Johnson-Bird clash sparked the phenomenal growth of the NCAA Final Four, which is now one of the most eagerly anticipated events on the sports calendar. The Johnson-Bird rivalry continued in the pros, and their memorable showdowns helped revive the NBA, which was struggling financially when the duo first joined the league. The 6'8" Johnson was a unique player in that he revolutionized the point guard position even though his frame was probably more suited to power forward. He set the all-time NBA record for assists and led the Los Angeles Lakers to five NBA titles during his career, which ended prematurely just before the 1991-92 season when he disclosed that he had contracted the HIV virus. Johnson attempted a few brief comebacks, including another stint with the Lakers during the second half of the 1995-96 season, but he retired once again after the team was knocked out of the playoffs. "Elizabeth Glaser [the late AIDS activist] said I was going to be around forever," Magic told *Sports Illustrated* in its Feb. 12, 1996 issue, shortly after announcing his latest comeback attempt. "She believed I would beat this, and I think she's right."

**Bob Martin**
*Brown Trix, Aintree Grand National,* 1989
Allsport/Bob Martin

**Mel Levine**
*New York City Marathon,* 1982
Sports Illustrated

**William Albert Allard**
*Dudley Field, El Paso, Texas,* 1990
National Geographic Society

**Lionel Cironneau**
*Greg LeMond, Tour de France*, 1990
AP/Wide World Photos
American Greg LeMond (yellow jersey) negotiates a curve in the final stage of the 1990 Tour de France. LeMond is the only American to win the hallowed race, and he did so three times (1986, '89 and '90) during a five-year period.

**Bob Martin**
*Whitbread Round the
World Yachting Race,*
1990
Allsport/Bob Martin

**Tim DeFrisco**
*Rollerbladers, Boulder, Colorado,* 1991
Allsport/Tim DeFrisco

**Mike Powell**
*Sepak Takraw, Foot
Volleyball, Malibu,
California,* 1991
Allsport/Mike Powell

**William Klein**
*Union Jack, British Fan, Torino,*
1990
©William Klein, Courtesy Howard
Greenberg Gallery, New York

**Jonathan Elderfield**
*From the series,*
*Dr. Dan—Marathon Man, #1, 1991*
© Jonathan Elderfield
On Nov. 3, 1991,
Dr. Daniel J. Winchester
finished the 26.2-mile
New York City Marathon in
11 hours and 20 minutes.
Winchester has cerebral palsy.
As a result, he must propel
himself backwards, using
only his legs and feet.

**Chris Hamilton**
*Wheelchair Racing,* 1991
© Chris Hamilton,
Atlanta, Georgia

**Jonathan Elderfield**
*From the series,*
*Dr. Dan—Marathon Man,*
*#2, 1991*
© Jonathan Elderfield

**Gary Newkirk**
*Ironman Triathlon in Hawaii*, 1991
Allsport/Gary Newkirk
This grueling competition was first organized in 1978 and has been held in Hawaii every year since. The race begins around 7 a.m. as competitors enter the water for a 2.4-mile swim. Next up is a 112-mile bike ride followed by a 26.2-mile run (the same distance as a marathon). It usually takes the winner a little more than eight hours to complete the race.

**Jose Azel**
*Ski Jump, Albertville Olympics,* 1992
Aurora

**Jun Tsukida**
*Rhythmic Gymnast with Ball,* 1991
Sasakawa Sports Foundation

**Jose Azel**
*Victor Petrenko, Albertville Olympics,* 1992
Aurora
Competing for the Unified Team at the 1992 Olympics in
Albertville, France, Victor Petrenko won the gold in men's figure
skating. He edged American Paul Wylie with a charismatic free
skate that included five triple jumps.

**Dave Black**
*Vitaly Scherbo, Barcelona Olympics,* 1992
© Dave Black
A native of Belarus, Vitaly Scherbo was a member of the Unified Team at the 1992 Games, where he won an unprecedented six gold medals in men's gymnastics (individual all-around, team competition, vault, parallel bars, pommel horse and rings).

**Chris Cole**
*Women's K-4 500-meter kayak race,*
*Barcelona Olympics,* 1992
Allsport/Chris Cole
Kayaks such as these, with four paddlers, move fast enough to pull a water skier. At the 1992 Games, Hungary, Germany and Sweden finished 1-2-3, respectively.

**Ken Geiger**
*Barcelona Olympics,* 1992
Dallas Morning News
While competing in a semifinal heat of the men's 400 meters at the 1992 Olympics in Barcelona, Great Britain's Derek Redmond collapsed to the track after tearing his right hamstring muscle. Sitting in the stands, Redmond's father watched his son's Olympic dreams disappear in an instant. But seeing his son writhe in agony was just too much to bear, so he somehow eluded security personnel and jumped over the barricade to get down on the track. Redmond had managed to stand, but his father embraced him and helped him to the finish line long after the race had ended. Still, the fans in Barcelona's Montjuïc Stadium cheered enthusiastically for Redmond's display of perseverance.

**Ken Geiger**

*Women's 4x100-meter relay team,
Barcelona Olympics,* 1992
Dallas Morning News
The Nigerian women celebrate as the
stadium scoreboard officially confirms
their surprising third-place finish.
African runners traditionally have
dominated long distance races,
but this was a rare bronze medal
in a sprint event.

**Ken Geiger**

*Olympic Soccer, Barcelona,* 1992
Dallas Morning News
Midfielder Cobi Jones (14) of the U.S. tries to head the ball despite
pressure from Italy's Mauro Bonomi. The Americans lost, 2-1, to the
heavily favored Italians but gained respect for keeping the game so
close. In fact, the U.S. actually dominated the game's final 45
minutes and almost tied the score on a shot by Jones, but it was
deflected over the crossbar of the goal.

**Chris Hamilton**
*Color Guard*, 1992
© Chris Hamilton, Atlanta, Georgia

**Rusty Kennedy**

*Jackie Joyner-Kersee, Barcelona,* 1992

AP/Wide World Photos

American Jackie Joyner-Kersee celebrates her victory in the heptathlon at the 1992 Games. It was her second straight Olympic title in this demanding event, which includes seven different competitions: 100-meter hurdles, high jump, shot put and 200-meter sprint on the first day; long jump, javelin and 800-meter run on the second. Her dominance in the heptathlon during the past decade—she set the world record of 7,291 points at the 1988 Games in Seoul—clearly established her as one of the greatest all-around athletes in history. Joyner-Kersee also won the long jump gold medal at the 1988 Games in Seoul, thus becoming the first athlete in 64 years to win golds in a multi-event and a single event at the same Olympics.

**Bob Martin**
*Scrambling at Touquet,*
*France,* 1992
Allsport/Bob Martin

**Birney Imes**
*Baseball*, 1993
© Birney Imes

**William Klein**
*Black Boxers, Paris*, 1992
© William Klein,
Courtesy Howard Greenberg Gallery,
New York

**Rich Clarkson**

*University of Texas Football,*
*Texas Stadium in Austin,* 1992
© Rich Clarkson

Texas running back Josh Sumner (35)
celebrates on the sidelines after the
Longhorns made yet another key play
during their stirring, come-from-
behind victory over Houston in 1992.
"Even though I came to UT as a
walk-on [no scholarship], I still feel
like an important part of the team,"
Sumner said. "You may not get
on the field as often as you would
like, but you can still help motivate
the guys. When you're on the
sidelines, you essentially become a
cheerleader. It's an unbelievable feel-
ing to be down there letting all your
emotions out. I wouldn't trade those
moments for anything in the world."

**Chris Hamilton**

*Martina Navratilova,* 1992
© Chris Hamilton, Atlanta, Georgia

Martina Navratilova retired from the pro tennis tour after the 1994
season having won more tournaments (167) than any other woman
in history (Chris Evert is second with 157). Her 54 Grand Slam
tournament victories rank second on the all-time list behind
Margaret Court (64), and she is tied with Chris Evert for the
third-most Grand Slam singles titles (18). Navratilova's impressive
résumé includes a record nine titles at Wimbledon, including a
string of six straight (1978, '79, '82-'87 and '90), four at the U.S.
Open (1983, '84, '86 and '87), three at the Australian Open (1981,
'83 and '85) and two at the French Open.

**Walter Iooss, Jr.**
*Anthony Mason, New York Knicks,* 1993
© Walter Iooss, Jr.
New York Knicks forward Anthony Mason is
one of the true rags-to-riches success stories
of the NBA. He didn't even play organized
basketball until his junior year at Springfield
Gardens High in the New York City borough
of Queens. After completing a largely
unnoticed college career at Tennessee
State, Mason struggled to make it as a pro,
traveling to such basketball outposts as
Turkey and Venezuela. He had brief stints
with the New Jersey Nets and the Denver
Nuggets before joining the New York Knicks
at the start of the 1991-92 NBA season.
Mason immediately became a fan favorite
at Madison Square Garden for his
hard-nosed style of play and won the
NBA's coveted Sixth Man award for the
1994-95 season. He became a starter
the following year and logged more minutes
than any other NBA player during the
1995-96 season. Mason is easily recognized
by the unique and ever-changing
messages he has shaved on his head.

**Stephen Dunn**
*Payne Stewart at Pebble
Beach,* 1993
Allsport/Stephen Dunn
Perhaps no golf course
in the world boasts the
incredible ocean vistas
of the famed Pebble
Beach in California. The
course was the site of
the U.S. Open in 1972,
1982 and 1992.

**Doug Acton**
*Mark Foo's Last Ride,* December 23, 1994
© Doug Acton
Hawaii's Mark Foo, an internationally known big-wave surfer, was tragically killed during this ride on the frigid waves at Mavericks, a spot south of San Francisco where swells often reach 30 feet.

**Andy Belcher**
*Agitator, South Island, New Zealand*, 1994
Sasakawa Sports Foundation

**Clive Brunskill**

*Yekaterina Gordeyeva and Sergei Grinkov, Pairs Skating,*
*Lillehammer Olympics, 1994*

Allsport/Clive Brunskill

G&G, as the husband-and-wife team was known to the skating community, won the gold in pairs skating at the 1994 Winter Games in Lillehammer, Norway, six years after winning their first Olympic gold at the 1988 Calgary Games. The two were considered the best pairs skaters ever and were universally adored by fans all over the world. They had skated together for nearly 14 years—since she was 11 and he was 15—when, during a routine practice session in Lake Placid, N.Y., in November 1995, Grinkov suddenly collapsed on the ice and died. Even though he had always kept himself in top shape, it was discovered he suffered from an undiagnosed case of coronary artery disease. Gordeyeva has vowed to continue skating, but she is adamant about not returning to pairs competition. "I cannot even think of someone else's arms around me, touching me," she told *Sports Illustrated*. "Since I was 11, I touched only Sergei's hand. Never anyone else's. This way I can still think of Sergei around me when I'm skating."

**Koichi Fujisaka**
*Ice Climbing*, 1994
Sasakawa Sports
Foundation

**Saburo Miyazaki**
*Parasailing*, 1994
Sasakawa Sports
Foundation

**Andy Hooper**
*Goalie Diving*, 1994
Sasakawa Sports Foundation

**Hiroaki Nagoshi**
*Sports arena at night,*
1994
Sasakawa Sports
Foundation

**Arthur Thill**
*F-1 Ablaze, Hockenheim Race Circuit, Germany, 1994*
© ATP/Arthur Thill

**Jay Koelzer**
*Kansas City Chiefs vs. Denver Broncos,*
1995
Allsport/Jay Koelzer

**David Burnett**

*Cal Ripken, Jr.,* Sept. 6, 1995

© David Burnett/Contact Press Images

In one of the most heartfelt ovations ever afforded an athlete, the fans at Camden Yards honor Baltimore Orioles shortstop Cal Ripken, Jr. for breaking Lou Gehrig's record of 2,130 consecutive games played. Gehrig's streak was once considered unreachable, but Ripken began his assault on May 29, 1982, and just kept going and going. Ripken is the only player in major league history to start in 12 consecutive All-Star games (no one else has a streak longer than 10). He also is the only player ever to win the MVP award the year after winning the Rookie of the Year award. And he already owns the record for most career home runs by a shortstop. But it is his bond with the fans that is truly special. "The Streak is going to end someday," said Bill Stetka, the Orioles' assistant director of publicity. "And when it does, it'll be because of a wrist injury from signing too many autographs."

# Afterword and Acknowledgments

This exhibition and book began to take form in 1990; its journey from conception to realization was a long and complex one. Without generous patronage, *Visions of Victory: A Century of Sports Photography* could not have been undertaken. We are especially honored to acknowledge our association with Champion International Corporation, The Paper Company. The support of Champion's John Hildenbiddle, Vice President, Creative Services, and Andy Sigler, Chief Executive Officer, have been extraordinary in every sense.

In the tasks of gathering and presenting so much diverse information, we have received generous assistance from many. First we want to thank our colleague Rich Clarkson and his staff members Emmett Jordan and Rick Garber. Rich, a distinguished photographer and photo editor, helped us invaluably to gain perspective on and access to the world of contemporary photographic sports journalism. Second, we wish to thank museum curator Frances Fralin, who, in the early stages of our compilation, brought her experience and taste to our task of amassing a body of images. Third, we wish to acknowledge the longstanding commitment to this exhibition of the Fernbank Museum of Natural History in Atlanta, where it is making its debut, and especially its Founding Director, Kay Davis. We also thank Fernbank staff members Kim Dunn, Melinda Chandler and Loretta Honea.

Our decision to blaze a new trail in the art of the photographic exhibition by using the Iris technology to print the entire exhibition was made easier by the presence in Washington, D.C., of David Adamson Editions. David's efforts in our behalf have gone far beyond the call of professionalism. His technical sophistication and personal goodwill have been equally appreciated. We also want to thank his associates, John Hughs and Laurie Hughs.

Two gifted design firms have brought their skills to the project: Alex Castro and Ingrid Castro of CastroArts in Baltimore have executed the design of the installation at Fernbank; Tina Davis of Tina Davis Design in New York, has designed the book. We are grateful to them, not only for their talent but for their hard work under short deadlines. We also thank Becky Pease of Frames By Rebecca and John Jacobs of Artex, who crated and shipped the exhibition.

One of the most important elements of any book about sports is that of the stories it tells about individual athletes. We are indebted to Joe Guise, Editor of Pindar Press, for researching and writing these anecdotal and historic entries. His expertise and lively writing style have added such an important element to this publication. We also want to acknowledge Pindar staff members Sonja Léobold, Cathy Sylvis, Shelly Gepfert, Richard Brescia and Jared Lipworth.

Of course no photographic exhibition can succeed without the creativity of the photographers whose work is included. To all of them, we express our admiration. For assistance in locating and providing their work, we want to acknowledge the following organizations and individuals: Sue Baldus, Allsport; Louis Andre, Jr.; Nat Andriani, AP/Wide World Photos; Martine d'Astier, Association des Amis de J.H. Lartigue; Chris Reid, Aurora: Ron Brenne, Bettmann Archive; Jeffrey Smith and Fiona McCaskie, Contact Press Images; James Danziger, James Danziger Gallery; Janice Madhu, George Eastman House; David Fahey, Fahey/Klein Gallery; Kathy Gailliot; Howard Greenberg and Carrie Springer, Howard Greenberg Gallery; Caroline Theakstone, Hulton Deutsch Collection; Monah Gettner, Hyperion Press; Connie McCabe; Ron Schmelzer, National Geographic Society; Gus Kayafas, Palm Press, Inc.; Tom Furusaka, Sasakawa Sports Foundation; Steve Gietschier, *The Sporting News*; Mike Dixon, *Sports Illustrated*; Abigail Silzer, Time-Life; and Joseph Walker and Paul McGinniss, Walker, Ursitti & McGinniss.

Finally, it is our hope that this unusual collaboration between our two entities—Jane Livingston Associates and Pindar Press—will pave the way for more such adventures, ours and others', based on the joining together of very different strengths in a spirit of mutual trust.

Dena Andre, Jane Livingston and Harvey Rubin